MW01326818

Media Center
Austin Middle School
3490 Ridge Road
Douglasville, GA 30134

LILLY SINGH

Actor and Comedian with More Than **3 BILLION VIEWS**

HENRIETTA TOTH

New York

For my niece Emi, who has taught me a lot about YouTube

Published in 2020 by The Rosen Publishing Group, Inc.
29 East 21st Street, New York, NY 10010

Copyright © 2020 by The Rosen Publishing Group, Inc.

First Edition

All rights reserved. No part of this book may be reproduced in any form without permission in writing from the publisher, except by a reviewer.

Library of Congress Cataloging-in-Publication Data

Names: Toth, Henrietta, author.
Title: Lilly Singh : actor and comedian with more than 3 billion views / Henrietta Toth.
Description: First edition. | New York : Rosen Publishing, 2020. | Series: Top YouTube stars | Includes bibliographical references and index.
Identifiers: LCCN 2019016391| ISBN 9781725348387 (library bound) | ISBN 9781725348370 (pbk.).
Subjects: LCSH: Singh, Lilly, 1988– Juvenile literature. | YouTube (Electronic resource)—Biography—Juvenile literature. | Internet personalities—United States—Biography—Juvenile literature. | Actors—United States—Biography—Juvenile literature. | Comedians—United States—Biography—Juvenile literature.
Classification: LCC PN1992.9236.S54 T68 2019 | DDC 791.092 [B]—dc23
LC record available at https://lccn.loc.gov/2019016391

Manufactured in the United States of America

On the cover: Lilly Singh appears at the 92nd Street Y in New York City on March 28, 2017, to discuss her book, *How to Be a Bawse: A Guide to Conquering Life.*

CONTENTS

INTRODUCTION 4

CHAPTER ONE
GROWING UP IN CANADA 7

CHAPTER TWO
IISUPERWOMANII 13

CHAPTER THREE
YOUTUBE SUPERSTAR 19

CHAPTER FOUR
UNICORN ISLAND 25

CHAPTER FIVE
BEYOND YOUTUBE 31

TIMELINE 38
GLOSSARY 40
FOR MORE INFORMATION 41
FOR FURTHER READING 42
BIBLIOGRAPHY 43
INDEX 47

INTRODUCTION

When Canadian YouTuber Lilly Singh was a child, she got a silver ring with the symbol "S" for Superman. It made her feel like a superhero, and it helped her get through some tough times while growing up. Singh could not know then that she would one day name her YouTube channel IISuperwomanII. Her successful channel has more than fourteen million subscribers and her videos have been viewed three billion times. In 2017, *Forbes* magazine listed Singh as one of the top ten entertainment influencers.

Singh is an actress, comedian, motivational speaker, rapper, and vlogger. In 2015, she performed her YouTube content during a worldwide concert tour. She called her tour A Trip to Unicorn Island. Singh is also a best-selling author. She published her book *How to Be a Bawse: A Guide to Conquering Life* in 2017. "Bawse" is a slang term for boss. Singh writes about focusing on the positive things in life. She explains her belief in harnessing one's confidence and drive to achieve things in life.

INTRODUCTION

Lilly Singh enthusiastically promotes her book *How to Be a Bawse: A Guide to Conquering Life* at her Los Angeles, California, book signing on May 1, 2017.

LILLY SINGH

Singh has a hectic schedule loading content on her YouTube channel, yet she finds time for philanthropic work. She was a UNICEF Goodwill Ambassador in 2018. She has also overcome personal challenges. Singh has shared with her YouTube viewers how she battled depression. In late 2018, Singh took a break from her YouTube channel. She was exhausted and needed a rest from preparing content for IISuperwomanII. However, within a month Singh returned to YouTube with some Christmas content. In January 2019, Singh posted a video explaining the changes she was making to her content and channel and called it the "evolution of Lilly." She looked forward to making 2019 the year to take risks and do new things, such as developing her production company and her own late-night television show.

CHAPTER ONE

Growing Up in Canada

Should she follow tradition or her own heart? That was the question facing Lilly Singh as she grew up. Lilly's parents had a traditional idea of how she should prepare for a career, while Lilly was searching for another way. As a child, Lilly was "that annoying kid at parties who would be at the center of a circle to get everyone's attention," she told Banu Ibrahim of AOL.com. As an adult, Singh found that her lively personality was the perfect fit for YouTube.

THE EARLY YEARS

Lilly Singh was born in Toronto, Canada, on September 26, 1988. She has one sister, Tina Singh, who is six years older. Tina is also a YouTuber. Her channel is called Mom Boss of 3 and she vlogs about her family and lifestyle. Tina has more than 80,000 subscribers, and her videos have four million views.

Lilly Singh poses with her parents at the 2016 premiere of her documentary, *A Trip to Unicorn Island*, in Los Angeles.

Lilly's parents are Malwinder and Sukhwinder Singh. They were wed in a traditionally arranged marriage in India. They emigrated to Canada from Punjab, a state in northern India. Lilly's father arrived in Canada in 1972 and her mother in 1981. After working in a series of jobs, Lilly's father acquired several gas stations. Lilly's parents bought a house in Malvern, and when she was sixteen, the family moved to Markham. Lilly was brought up in a traditional Sikh household, where they practiced the Sikh religion. Sikhism began five hundred years ago and is the fifth largest religion in the world. Sikhs believe in serving God and others. Many Sikh men do not cut their hair or beards and wear turbans on their heads. Some women also wear turbans or cover their hair with scarves.

A TOMBOY

Singh admits to being a tomboy when she was growing up. She loved attention and she already enjoyed performing as a child. In fact, from an early age, Lilly wanted to be an actress or a rapper. When she was eight years old, Lilly lugged around a camcorder to film herself whenever she thought of a dance move or skit.

In the third grade, Lilly was obsessed with the wrestler called the Rock. She had a cardboard cutout of the Rock in her room and even dressed like him. Lilly's obsession with the wrestler was well known at her school. In the sixth grade, Lilly gave her classmates the Rock-themed cards on Valentine's Day. If school officials called her over the intercom, they would say Lilly "the Rock" Singh. Lilly never could have imagined as a girl that one day her YouTube career would lead her to meet the Rock, whose real name is Dwayne Johnson (now an actor and producer).

Making a heart symbol for her fans, Lilly Singh attends WE Day, which empowers young people to make a difference, in Inglewood, California, on April 7, 2016.

THE COLLEGE YEARS

In 2006, Lilly graduated from high school, the Lester B. Pearson Collegiate Institute in Scarborough. She started college that fall at York University, majoring in psychology. Often, instead of studying, Singh choreographed Punjabi dance shows at school. After college, Singh's parents wanted her to go to graduate school and earn a master's degree in counseling psychology. But Singh was not happy preparing for graduate school and a traditional

SOME THINGS TO KNOW ABOUT SINGH

Her Favorite Foods
   Singh loves popcorn smothered with extra butter. If she's having a bad day, a serving of macaroni and cheese can make the day seem better. Her favorite candy is Skittles, and she likes to have plenty of it around. One food that Singh doesn't like is tomatoes.

Her Favorite Shows
   Singh is a fan of the HBO series *Game of Thrones*. When she was growing up, her favorite show was *The Simpsons*. Singh doesn't like the movie *The Lion King* because she finds the story upsetting.

Things That Singh Likes
   Singh likes IKEA furniture and bright colors. She uses both to decorate her new home in Los Angeles, California.

Things That Singh Doesn't Like
   Singh is afraid of creepy crawly spiders. She has been afraid of clowns ever since she saw the Stephen King movie *It*. She also has a fear of commitment.

The Special Meanings of Singh's Tattoos
   A tattoo on her collarbone reads "One Love," Singh's message to the world. On the insides of her wrists are two Punjabi words: *Nirbhao*, which means "without fear," and *Nirvair*, which means "without hate."

career path in life. Singh found the "idea of living this linear life—take classes, go to grad school, get a job" depressing, as she explained to Emily Landau of *Toronto Life*. Singh found some relief from her depression in the Sikh religion. She also decided to take a year off after graduating college in 2010.

DISCOVERING YOUTUBE

One day, during this year off after college, Singh came across YouTube on the internet. She watched a video posted by Jenna

DEPRESSION

Depression is a type of mental health or mood disorder. It is quite common, and more than three million cases are diagnosed in the United States each year. One in five people a year are affected in Canada. More girls and women struggle with depression than boys or men. Well-known people who have battled depression include US president Abraham Lincoln, authors Charles Dickens and J. K. Rowling, actress Selena Gomez, and singers Alicia Keys and Lady Gaga.

Symptoms of depression include a lack of feeling and of hope. People who suffer from depression report being sad all the time. They also lose interest in the things they once enjoyed and sometimes think about suicide. These symptoms can affect the whole body through changes in eating and sleeping patterns and weight loss or gain. Depression is treated with medication, such as antidepressants, and by talking to a therapist.

YouTuber Jenna Marbles and her dog Kermit appear on the YouTube show *What's Trending* on July 9, 2013, in Hollywood, California.

Marbles. Marbles is a comedian and actress who creates video satires for her YouTube channel, JennaMarbles. Marbles was one of the first YouTubers to draw viewers based on her personality instead of a specific theme. In one week, an early video that Marbles uploaded attracted more than five million views.

Singh was amazed by what she saw on JennaMarbles. "I didn't realize that you could create that kind of content on YouTube," she told Emily Landau of *Toronto Life*. Singh recorded her first video for YouTube the very next day. It was not the funny material that has made Singh a YouTube star. It was a serious monologue about the place that religion had in her life at that time, and seventy people viewed it. Singh has since deleted it because she thought it was poorly done.

Singh was now bitten by the YouTube bug. She bought a camera on sale and began filming and uploading videos from her bedroom in her parents' house in Markham, Canada. Her parents doubted that Singh could make this nontraditional career path work, but they gave Singh a year to try it. Singh was now on her way to becoming a first-generation Canadian success story.

CHAPTER TWO

IISuperwomanII

Singh made a deal with her parents that she would try YouTube for a year or go back to graduate school. But she was determined to make her living her way. Like a superwoman, "for that year, I just really, really hustled," she said in an interview with Banu Ibrahim of AOL.com.

"WHADDUP!"

In October 2010, Singh launched and began building her YouTube channel using the pseudonym IISuperwomanII. Singh received permission from the comic book publisher DC Comics to use the Superwoman trademark. "Superwoman" was also the name of a rap song that Singh liked. Singh started posting videos that open with her excitedly greeting her viewers with "Whaddup!" and a hand signal "S" for Superwoman. The "S" is also a signal for Scarborough, a section of Toronto, Canada, where Singh grew up.

Lilly Singh poses by her art installation *Girl Love* on opening night at the exhibit *29Rooms* in Los Angeles, California, on December 6, 2017.

Singh likes having control over her material as she develops content for her channel. She likes being her own boss. She plans, writes, directs, films, stars in, and edits her own videos. Along the way, Singh has learned a lot about the process through trial and error. Her performances are full of energy, and she often plays more than one character.

Singh gives credit to YouTube for saving her from a traditional career and life path that she did not want. She says YouTube also helped her find herself and lift her depression. "Talking about really silly things I got my personality back. Growing up I was the life of the party, I was that silly goofy kid. And then I went through this rough time and kind of lost myself. Discovering YouTube was actually the best thing that ever happened to me," she explained to Casey Lewis of *Teen Vogue*.

"IT'S YOUR GIRL, SUPERWOMAN!"

The image of Singh's Superwoman character is that of a gruff and untidy tomboy. Singh dresses in large flannel shirts and wears baseball caps backward. She also likes fun clothes like colorful hats and weird shoes. She wears things that make her happy and

SINGH'S MOST POPULAR QUOTES (FROM OPENQUOTES)

"Love who you are, embrace who you are. Love yourself. When you love yourself, people can kind of pick up on that: they can see confidence, they can see self-esteem, and naturally, people gravitate towards you."

"Life is designed to knock you down. It will knock you down time and time again, but it doesn't matter how many times you fall—it matters how many times you get back up."

"I've discovered home is not a place anymore. It's the people around you."

"You need a really solid foundation of friends and family to keep you where you need to be."

"Everyone's voice should be heard when it comes to racial barriers."

"There's no escalators—there's only staircases to success. There is no substitute for hard work."

"You can do anything you want."

reflect her personality. Singh talks in a loud voice peppered with slang. She uses comedy to deliver her content and information. Much of Singh's early material appealed to teens, especially girls of South Asian heritage. She filmed a series of parodies about parents using her Punjabi parents as examples. Her video "Types of Parents" received more than ten million views. She even posted an instructional video on how to wrap a Sikh turban.

Another popular video, with nearly thirty million views, is "How Girls Get Ready," which shows Singh painting her nails, deciding what to wear, showering, and putting on makeup over several hours. Other topics on IISuperwomanII are about hair, exams, and school crushes. Singh has also posted content ranting about things that she doesn't like, like flying and going through restaurant drive-throughs. In 2014, Singh added a music video

Fans pose for selfies with Lilly Singh at YouTube Brandcast, an advertising event in New York City on May 5, 2016.

IISUPERWOMANII 17

to her channel that gained more than twelve million views. It was the official video for the song "#LEH," which is slang for "ugh" or "whatever." Singh recorded the song with her friend Humble the Poet, who is also a Sikh Canadian YouTuber, author, and rapper.

Most important to Singh is to include in her content observations about life that inspire and motivate her audience. She says that her own inspiration comes from her real-life experiences. Plus, she believes in the need to love oneself and stay positive in order to succeed in anything.

A UNIQUE APPROACH

When Singh was developing her YouTube brand and platform, she decided to include her audience by tapping into their minds

HOW TO START A YOUTUBE CHANNEL

The influence and popularity of YouTube continues to grow. More than thirty million people around the world check YouTube every day for new content. It's easy to film a video on a smartphone, edit it on a laptop, and then upload it to a channel.

The YouTube website has instructions on starting a channel that are simple to follow. First, think about who your audience will be. Who will you be making these videos for? Check out competing videos by other YouTubers to see if you can do anything differently. Then, film your first video and set up your channel. Use a title for your video that is easy to find on Google. Finally, set up a schedule to produce new content and videos to post to your channel each week.

LILLY SINGH

and emotions. Unlike many mainstream Hollywood artists who keep their audience at a distance, Singh talks directly to her viewers and gains their trust and following. She also lets her audience see her imperfections as she embraces them and pokes fun at them. She is not afraid to point out the pimple that popped out on her face or to admit that she's having a bad hair day. She takes everyday situations that everybody goes through and can relate to, then puts a comic spin on them. Her viewers see that even though everyone's different, they're also the same. Singh sees her YouTube channel as a way to make herself and others smile, laugh, and be happy.

By 2011, Singh's ||Superwoman|| channel had several thousand subscribers. She had a strong following, especially among the South Asian community. Singh's videos made her famous and she was recognized on the street and in stores by her fans.

MAKING A LIVING

Singh found a purpose in developing content for YouTube. But could she develop the career she wanted and make a salary doing it? As Singh's visibility rose on YouTube, other YouTubers reached out to her. One in particular showed Singh that it was possible to make a living through YouTube. Allen Buckle, known as Fluffee Talks, is also a Canadian YouTuber. He finds the funny side in the odd news stories and videos that he posts on his channel. Singh met Buckle at his house and asked him what he does. "I do YouTube," he said. "I bought this house with money from making videos," Singh recalled in an interview with Emily Landau of *Toronto Life*. Singh said she "was blown away. I had no idea people could make a living posting videos."

CHAPTER THREE

YouTube Superstar

Once Singh realized that she might be able to make a living doing YouTube, she put all her energy into IISuperwomanII. Her hard work started to pay off. The number of followers and views on her channel grew. She was on her way to becoming a YouTube superstar.

BUILDING IISUPERWOMANII

Singh focused on building her YouTube brand and getting into the routine of running her channel. She started posting content on a regular basis. Singh kept a strict and hectic schedule. Every Monday and Thursday, she uploaded new content and videos. Singh continues to work hard on her YouTube career. She admits she's a workaholic and likes to be productive. "I think about Superwoman and what to do next all the time," she told Karishma Upadhyay of asiaone.com. Singh further explained to Sneha Mankani of *Vogue India*, "I love what I do so much. If

LILLY SINGH

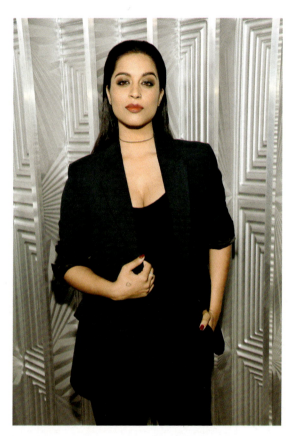

Lilly Singh takes part in *ELLE* magazine's 24th Annual Women in Hollywood Celebration in Beverly Hills, California, on October 16, 2017.

not recording, I'm writing scripts, attending to emails, having meetings or working on marketing tactics."

For her videos, Singh has developed characters that are almost as well-known as she is. Singh portrays people and situations that viewers can relate to. She does this using a variety of genres but mostly parody and satire. Singh also collaborates with other performers. Some of her favorite characters are her Punjabi parents, who criticize her choices and think they know what's best for her. She also likes the kid, the jerk, and the bimbo.

In December 2011, Singh started her vlog channel called Superwoman Vlogs. The channel has grown to nearly three million subscribers. Singh says her vlog is like writing in a diary. She posts about the day-to-day things in her life, which sometimes can be boring, and about her thoughts and feelings. Singh explains that her vlog channel is more about real life. Her main channel, IISuperwomanII, is more of a performance. Singh also posts more personal happenings on her Twitter account, @IISuperwomanII.

TEAM SUPER

Singh's die-hard followers are called Team Super. They are also called Unicorns because Singh is obsessed with the mythical horned animal. Singh's followers can buy IISuperwomanII merchandise from her website. The IISuperwomanII brand is on items such as hats, hoodies, and T-shirts. By 2012, one hundred thousand people were following IISuperwomanII. In two years, that number reached one million followers. Her audience was mostly young women between the ages of sixteen and twenty-four.

Singh realized the extent of her growing fame in 2014 when she attended the YouTube FanFest in Mumbai, India. Several famous YouTubers performed at this event. It was Singh's first trip overseas. She met Bollywood star Shah Rukh Khan and shared the stage with him before two thousand screaming fans. Singh couldn't believe it and told Emily Landau of *Toronto Life*, "I felt sick for the rest of the night. I was shaking. I didn't know how to deal with it." By 2016, Singh had become one of YouTube's

Bollywood star Shah Rukh Khan speaks about his superhero film *Ra.One* at the YouTube media meet in Mumbai, India, on September 26, 2011.

VIDEO POSTING TIPS

Singh has successfully posted content to her channel for several years. She has learned what does and doesn't work. So, she can suggest these tips for anyone building a YouTube career.

1. Create content that matters. If the topic is something that you care about, there are probably others who will also care. Don't create content just to gain internet fame.
2. Create positive content. Stay away from negative topics that might hurt or offend others.
3. Create content that shows your personality and uniqueness. Viewers want to have a connection and know who is creating the content.
4. Don't spend time overthinking or worrying about content, but do plan it out. It takes time and work to create good content.
5. Create content on a regular schedule so that fans know what days and times to tune in.
6. Ignore negative comments. Not everyone will like every type of content. Plus, some viewers just like to leave nasty comments.

highest earning performers. *Forbes* magazine listed her as the third-highest-earning YouTuber that year, earning US $7.5 million.

MOVING TO LOS ANGELES

As Singh's career continued to expand, she started taking creative meetings in Los Angeles, California. Sometimes, she flew there twice a month. She was finding it difficult to prepare video

YOUTUBE SUPERSTAR 23

content from her parents' house in Markham, Canada. Finally, Singh decided to move to Los Angeles to further her career. In 2015, Singh bought a house in a Los Angeles neighborhood called Hancock Park. She decorated it in the vibrant colors she loves. To her home library, she added books by other YouTube stars, such as Hannah Hart, Grace Helbig, and Tyler Oakley. Most important, Singh designed a production studio in which to film her videos and content.

It was the first time that Singh was out on her own and she was scared at first. She had to learn how to pay the bills and do laundry. But she settled into her new home and made friends in Hollywood quickly: for example, Selena Gomez appeared on Singh's Instagram page and in a video for her vlog.

Lilly Singh wins for Best First-Person Series at the 5th Annual Streamy Awards, held in Los Angeles, California, on September 17, 2015.

SPONSORS OF IISUPERWOMANII

The main sources of income for YouTubers are advertisements and subscriptions to their channels. Singh's channel is sponsored by brands, such as Coca-Cola and Toyota, which advertise their products. The sponsors then promote Singh's content through

LOS ANGELES, THE YOUTUBE CAPITAL

Los Angeles (LA) has long been the film capital of the world. It is also a media capital, where there are many opportunities for YouTubers to attend creative meetings and events. One such large event is VidCon. This convention has been held each year since 2010 in Southern California. Creators of online videos of all genres attend, as well as viewers and media representatives.

Many successful YouTubers move to LA to further their careers. They can take advantage of better production facilities to film more professional looking content. LA is also a great place to meet and work with other YouTubers. When YouTubers collaborate on content, it draws more viewers to their channels. Some YouTubers develop their craft beyond the video-sharing website. They move into mainstream Hollywood to pursue acting or stand-up comedy.

their ads aimed at her young audience. Singh even appears in some of the ads. She promotes a deep-red lipstick developed by Smashbox cosmetics named "Bawse" in her honor.

However, not everyone can make the kind of living that Singh does from YouTube. Singh is successful because of her content. It attracts viewers, which in turn attracts brand sponsorships. In an interview with Jessy Bains of Yahoo Finance Canada, author Mark W. Schaefer explains, "It's a function of creating exceptional, entertaining content that people want to see every day. The only way Lilly Singh made it to the top and stayed there was to be consistently interesting and earning that audience every day." Viewers tune in regularly because Singh is consistently funny, original, and uplifting.

CHAPTER FOUR

Unicorn Island

As Singh's success increased, she looked for new ways to expand her performance and express her artistry. She wanted to branch out from her weekly uploads to YouTube. Singh had already performed on stage with other YouTubers at

A unicorn gets a kiss from Lilly Singh at the VidCon celebration in Anaheim, California, on June 23, 2016.

media events. So, she took the next step by performing her content in front of an audience of her fans.

A HAPPY PLACE

For Singh, the definition of a happy place is Unicorn Island. "I always call Unicorn Island a synonym for my happy place, so Unicorn Island means someone's happy place," she explained to Deepa Lakshmin of *MTV News*. Unicorn Island is a place that has helped Singh battle depression, lack of confidence, and fear. It's a place where there is only happiness. Singh often reminds her fans to fight for their own happiness.

Singh named her happy place after the unicorns she loves so much. They also represent her expanding career—it's why she named her world tour A Trip to Unicorn Island.

ON THE ROAD

Singh launched her first world tour in March 2015. She took her YouTube content on the road to sold-out arenas and stadiums. She performed in twenty-seven cities in several countries, including Australia, Canada, England, India, and the United States. When Rega Jha of *BuzzFeed* asked Singh why people should come to see her live she responded, "It'll remind you how awesome life is!"

Singh especially looked forward to meeting her fans. "There's something about seeing people's faces, and it's amazing [seeing how] things online can also be translated offline," she described to Deepa Lakshmin of *MTV News*. Singh was overwhelmed by the wonderful and unexpected reception she received in India. A

UNICORN ISLAND 27

Fans meet with Lilly Singh at the opening of her movie *A Trip to Unicorn Island* at the TCL Chinese Theatre in Los Angeles, California, on February 10, 2016.

lot of work, such as planning and rehearsals, went into the show. It was a high-energy performance of comedy, singing, dancing, and rapping with a cast of backup dancers. Singh also talked to her audience about the importance of happiness. She invited them to her own personal place of happiness, Unicorn Island. Although the tour was exhausting, Singh says it was an amazing experience.

The successful tour was documented on film so that all of Singh's fans could see it. YouTube Premium (formerly YouTube Red) provided financing and promotion for the tour. YouTube Premium is an offshoot of YouTube that produces original content. *A Trip to Unicorn Island* was released in 2016 on YouTube Red.

THE GOOD AND THE BAD OF YOUTUBE

A good thing about YouTube is that it is a reliable platform for uploading creative, entertaining, or educational content. It accepts homemade videos as well as professional ones. Most content can be created inexpensively. YouTube reaches a large audience all over the world. Some YouTubers can make a living through their channel.

A bad thing about YouTube is the pressure YouTubers often feel to produce and upload content to their channel on schedule. There's also pressure to keep their content fun and interesting for fans. Being a YouTube celebrity can sometimes get tiring, and some YouTubers suffer from burnout. It's important to avoid revealing personal information in order to stay safe. Remember that fake views of a channel can inflate the real number of people watching it and that making a living as a YouTuber is not guaranteed.

ONWARD AND UPWARD

Although Singh's YouTube channel is successful, she continues to work on improving it and learning from her mistakes. She analyzes which videos do well or don't. She also credits viewer comments with helping her to develop content. Singh has a specific vision for her videos and works on improving their look through better production values.

As Singh has gained a more diverse following, she has expanded her material beyond South Asian themes to more general and relatable topics. She's reached out to teens and people

SINGH'S YOUTUBE COLLABORATORS

Many successful YouTubers collaborate on the content they load onto their channels. They blend their ideas to come up with new and creative material that will appeal to all their fans. The YouTube community enjoys working together. Plus, collaborating on material brings more viewers to their individual channels.

Singh's success has given her the opportunity to collaborate with YouTubers Grace Helbig, Humble the Poet, and Jenna Marbles. Mainstream Hollywood actors like Dwayne "the Rock" Johnson, Selena Gomez, and Will Smith have done skits with Singh on her videos. Collaborations are important to Singh, and she takes them seriously. She puts a lot of effort into matching the right material to the right collaborator because she wants to produce the best possible product.

of all backgrounds with her content. By 2016, Singh had doubled her subscribers to six million.

With great success comes more work and responsibility. Singh realized that she needed help to manage her channel, so she signed with a manager. Plus, Hollywood was taking notice of Singh. She began appearing on talk shows doing her comedy and other content from her channel. Singh is a star made in reverse. She did it on her own with YouTube. Now mainstream Hollywood performers, such as Ariana Grande and Seth Rogen, appear in Singh's videos and she has collaborated with several other celebrities.

AWARDS AND RECOGNITION

Lilly Singh appears onstage at the 2017 Streamy Awards, held at the Hilton Hotel in Beverly Hills, California, on September 26, 2017.

Early in her career, Singh started to win recognition for IISuperwomanII. In 2014, her YouTube channel came in at number thirty-nine on the list of New Media Rockstars Top 100. The September 2015 issue of *People* magazine added Singh to its list of "Ones to Watch." Awards soon followed, with Singh winning the 2015 MTV Fandom Award for Social Superstar of the Year. Since then, she's been nominated for and won more awards. In 2016, Singh was the winner of the female Choice Web Star in the Teen Choice Awards. Singh has also won four Streamy Awards, including one for *A Trip to Unicorn Island*, the film of her world tour. In 2017, she was voted Favorite YouTube Star by the People's Choice Award.

Singh enjoys going to award shows and says she finds them inspiring. She has fun dressing up for the shows and walking the red carpet. Singh has thanked Team Super when she's won saying, "We won a Streamy." She explained to Deepa Lakshmin of *MTV News*, "We is Team Super, my Unicorns, and that's simply because if Team Super didn't watch my videos, we wouldn't have that Streamy, and I want to pay tribute to that. My favorite thing about YouTube is that it makes community."

CHAPTER FIVE

Beyond YouTube

In addition to her work on YouTube, Singh has other areas where she's been developing her talents. She has written two books, reworked her IISuperwomanII channel, and has moved into mainstream Hollywood projects. Plus, Singh has taken part in humanitarian causes like the #GirlLove campaign.

A BEST-SELLING AUTHOR

Singh can add best-selling author to her list of accomplishments. Her book *How to Be a Bawse: A Guide to Conquering Life* was released on March 28, 2017. It is partly a memoir and partly a self-help and motivational book. Singh writes about ways people can project confidence and reach their goals. She launched the book on a tour, making thirty stops across the globe from New York to Hong Kong. On May 16, 2017, *How to Be a Bawse* made the *New York Times* best-seller list.

Lilly Singh speaks at the Room to Read International Day of the Girl, promoting literacy and education, in San Francisco, California, on October 11, 2018.

On April 22, 2017, Singh released another book: *Toxic Relationships: How to De-Tox from Negative People and Abusive Relationships.* In this short guide, Singh discusses ways to improve your life by ridding it of toxic people.

PHILANTHROPIC WORK

Singh's philanthropic work is important to her, and it also keeps her busy. In 2016, Singh started the #GirlLove campaign to stop girl-on-girl hatred and bullying. "The sad reality is that girl-on-girl hate is such a big issue in schools, at work, or online," Singh explained to Sam Gutelle of tubefilter.com. She even met with

SINGH THE AUTHOR

Singh's first book, *How to Be a Bawse: A Guide to Conquering Life,* is a guide to taking control of your life by projecting confidence with a smile and working hard. Based on her own journey in her life and YouTube career, Singh writes down her insights to inspire and help others. She includes chapters with advice like not overthinking, exercising self-control, committing to decisions, eliminating stress, and appreciating things. But Singh also reminds her readers that there is no secret to a rewarding life and that the worthwhile things in life take time. Included are funny photos of Singh and comic illustrations.

Michelle Obama at the White House to discuss the campaign and gather support for it. To raise awareness, Singh designed a bracelet displaying the ME to WE logo. Several of Singh's fellow female YouTubers, including comedian Grace Helbig and violinist Lindsey Stirling, helped promote #GirlLove. The 2016 Streamy Award for Social Good was given to Singh for the campaign.

In 2018, Singh served as a UNICEF Goodwill Ambassador, working on behalf of children's rights and education. Singh went to South Africa to meet with elementary school students who speak out on bullying and school violence.

Also in 2018, Singh appeared in ads for the Face Anything campaign developed by Olay beauty products. Appearing in the September 2018 issue of *Vogue* magazine, these ads featured diverse women who are bold enough to follow their ambitions and not apologize for being successful. The Face Anything campaign fit Singh's personal aim of empowering young women to achieve their goals by watching her own career journey.

LILLY SINGH

UN Goodwill Ambassador Lilly Singh displays a UNICEF T-shirt during a press conference in New Delhi, India, on July 15, 2017.

"I'LL SEE YOU SOON"

Singh took a break from YouTube in November 2018. "I am mentally, physically, emotionally, and spiritually exhausted," she explained in a video posted to her channel. She described how she had been working on IISuperwomanII for the past eight years and needed a rest and to work on her mental health, including her state of happiness. However, Singh said that taking a break did not mean she no longer loved YouTube or Team Super. She just wanted to step back and rethink her content and the direction she wanted it to take. Plus, Singh needed time and energy to work on her projects outside of YouTube, like her production company. Singh's fans responded with support and said they awaited her return to the internet.

RETURN TO YOUTUBE

In early December 2018, Singh made an ambitious and triumphant comeback to YouTube. She posted *12 Collabs of*

SINGH AND HER CRITICS

While Singh's fans find her content inspiring and her videos funny, some people think she is overrated and that her performances are over the top. Singh realizes that not everyone will like her material or the way she presents it. Sometimes negative comments do get to her, even though she says she has a thick skin. Singh just tries to focus on the positive in the face of online hate and has spoken out against internet trolls.

Some YouTubers have made negative comments about Singh. PewDiePie called Singh a crybaby when Singh observed that there weren't any women on *Forbes* magazine 2018 list of richest YouTubers. Singh responded by clarifying her remarks that she was simply stating a fact.

Christmas videos in which she collaborated with entertainers such as Charlize Theron, Will Smith, and singers Nick Jonas and John Legend. Then, in her video posted on January 9, 2019, Singh exclaimed "This channel is changing!" She explained the changes she was making to her channel and content. She dropped the Superwoman name and would be going by her name Lilly. Her schedule for uploading videos would be less rigid, and she would spend more time on developing her material and post topics as they came to her. Most important, Singh would focus on her own happiness, and she encouraged her viewers to do the same. "I always say that fighting for your happiness is the most important thing you'll ever fight for," she said. On February 24, 2019, Singh made news with the tweet that

Lilly Singh models her gown at the Met Gala fundraiser at the Metropolitan Museum of Art in New York City on May 6, 2019.

she's bisexual, as well as female and colored. Her tweet was met with positive responses from many fans for opening up discussions and recognition of lesbian, gay, bisexual, and transgender (LGBT) issues within the South Asian LGBT community.

ON TO HOLLYWOOD

Now that Singh has conquered YouTube, she is ready to take on Hollywood. She became successful in the entertainment world by working hard at her craft and forging her own path. Singh

BEYOND YOUTUBE 37

continues to look toward the future by developing projects on and off YouTube. Plus, she hopes to reach an audience beyond the internet. She's trying new things, such as running her own production company. Singh is also looking for more opportunities to act, and she already has some acting credits. She played Raven in the 2018 HBO production of *Fahrenheit 451*. Earlier, she voiced the characters Misty and Bubbles in the 2016 film *Ice Age: Collision Course*.

Singh has appeared on talk shows such as *The Tonight Show Starring Jimmy Fallon*. And in 2019 she landed her own talk show called *A Little Late with Lilly Singh*. Singh is the first woman of color and openly bisexual female to host a late-night talk show. The program will be "kind of like my YouTube channel," she told Agence France-Presse of *The Jakarta Post*. "I think it's a little awesome for an Indian Canadian woman to be on a late-night show," she added.

So, although Singh has dropped the Superwoman name from her channel, she continues to prove that she can be super at whatever she tries.

TIMELINE

- **1988** Singh is born on September 26 in Toronto, Canada.
- **2004** Singh and her family move to Markham, a city outside of Toronto.
- **2006** Singh graduates from high school, the Lester B. Pearson Collegiate Institute.
- **2010** Singh graduates from York University in Toronto; she takes a year off after college and posts her first video; she launches her YouTube channel, IISuperwomanII, in October.
- **2011** IISuperwomanII gains several thousand subscribers; Singh launches a second YouTube channel, Superwoman Vlogs.
- **2014** Singh receives her first award nomination for a Shorty Award as YouTube Comedian; she attends the YouTube FanFest in Mumbai, India; she posts the music video for her song "#LEH" with Humble the Poet.
- **2015** Beginning in March, Singh takes her YouTube content on the road in a world tour; she wins the MTV Fandom Award for Social Superstar; she moves to Los Angeles in December.
- **2016** Singh launches the #GirlLove campaign; she wins a Streamy Award for Social Good; *A Trip to Unicorn Island*, a documentary of her world tour, is released; she voices the characters Misty and Bubbles in the film *Ice Age: Collision Course*; she wins the Teen Choice Award for Web Star: Comedy; *Forbes* magazine lists Singh as the third-highest-earning YouTuber; she has six million subscribers.

TIMELINE

2017 *How to Be a Bawse: A Guide to Conquering Life* is published on March 28; Singh wins the People's Choice Award as Favorite YouTube Star.

2018 Singh serves as a UNICEF Goodwill Ambassador; she plays Raven in the HBO television film *Fahrenheit 451*; she takes a break from YouTube in November; she returns to IISuperwomanII with Christmas content.

2019 On January 9, Singh posts her changes to her channel, including dropping the Superwoman name; she announces on Twitter that she is bisexual; she gets her own late-night talk show.

GLOSSARY

bawse Slang term for boss.
Bollywood The name for the movie industry in India.
brand The identity or image that promotes something.
choreograph To arrange steps or moves for a performance.
collaborate To work together on a project or activity.
first-generation The generation born in the country to which their parents immigrated.
genre Things grouped together by a similar form or style.
memoir The story of someone's emotions and memories.
monologue A speech given by one person.
offshoot Something that developed from a main product.
parody A usually funny imitation of someone or something.
philanthropy Donating or raising money for a worthy cause.
platform Bringing attention to one's work through social media and other methods.
pseudonym A name, other than one's own, used for a specific purpose.
Punjab A state in northern India.
satire A comical exaggeration of a person or thing.
Sikh A religion that is practiced in the Punjab state.
therapist A professional person who treats psychological problems.
trademark A symbol that identifies a particular brand or merchandise.
turban A cloth wound around the head that is usually worn by Sikh men.

FOR MORE INFORMATION

Creative Stand Up: Comedy with Personality
Website: http://creativestandup.com
Courses and tips on building a comedy routine are offered on this website.

IMDB (Lilly Singh's page)
Website: https://www.imdb.com/name/nm6530360
Singh's page on the movie, TV, and video online database IMDB has trivia, quotes, and photos.

Lilly Singh
Website: https://www.youtube.com/channel/UCfm4y4rHF5HGrSr-qbvOwOg
Singh's @IISuperwomanII YouTube channel has videos of her comedy skits, impersonations of people, and collaborations with other YouTubers and artists.

Lilly Singh Official Website
Website: http://lillysingh.com
Facebook, Instagram, and Twitter: @IISuperwomanII
YouTube: @IISuperwomanII
Singh's website and social media accounts include information, photos, and merchandise like Team Super apparel.

Lilly Singh Vlogs
YouTube: @SuperwomanVlogs
This YouTube channel has daily uploads and video extras on more personal topics.

YouTube
901 Cherry Avenue
San Bruno, CA 94066
(650) 253-0000
Website: http://www.youtube.com
Facebook, Twitter, and Instagram: @YouTube
YouTube is a video-sharing American website founded in 2005. It is now part of Google.

YouTube Spotlight Canada
YouTube: @ YouTube Spotlight Canada
Source for Canadian creators of YouTube content that focuses on the culture and trends affecting Canada.

FOR FURTHER READING

Berry, Jo. *Lilly Singh: The Unofficial Superwoman Guide.* London, UK: Trapeze Books, 2017.

Furgang, Adam. *Jenna Marbles: Comedian with More Than 2 Billion Views.* New York, NY: Rosen Publishing, 2019.

Furgang, Adam. *20 Great Career-Building Activities Using YouTube.* New York, NY: Rosen Publishing, 2017.

Grabham, Tim. *Video Ideas: Full of Awesome Ideas to Try Out Your Video-Making Skills.* New York, NY: DK Children, 2018.

Hall, Kevin. *Creating and Building Your Own YouTube Channel.* New York, NY: Rosen Publishing, 2017.

Juilly, Brett. *Make Your Own Amazing YouTube Videos: Learn to Film, Edit, and Upload Quality Videos to YouTube.* New York, NY: Skyhorse Publishing, 2017.

McAneney, Caitie. *Online Safety: Let's Talk About It.* New York, NY: Rosen Publishing, 2015.

Singh, Lilly. *How to Be a Bawse: A Guide to Conquering Life.* New York, NY: Ballantine Books, 2017.

Tashjian, Janet, and Jake Tashjian. *My Life as a YouTuber.* New York, NY: Henry Holt and Co., 2018.

Willoughby, Nick. *Digital Filmmaking for Kids.* Hoboken, NJ: John Wiley & Sons, 2015.

Willoughby, Nick. *Making YouTube Videos: Star in Your Own Video.* Hoboken, NJ: John Wiley & Sons, 2015.

BIBLIOGRAPHY

@IISuperwomanII. "√Female √Coloured √Bisexual…" Twitter, February 24, 2019. https://twitter.com/IISuperwomanII/status/1099837949951111168.

Bains, Jessy. "'$65,000 per Sponsored YouTube': Lilly Singh Made a Ton Before Her Late Night Gig." Yahoo Finance Canada, March 15, 2019. https://finance.yahoo.com/news/65000-per-sponsored-you-tube-post-lilly-singh-made-a-ton-before-her-late-night-gig-191144635.html.

Berg, Madeline. "The Highest-Paid YouTube Stars 2016: PewDiePie Remains No. 1 with $15 Million." *Forbes*, December 20, 2016. https://www.forbes.com/sites/maddieberg/2016/12/05/the-highest-paid-youtube-stars-2016-pewdiepie-remains-no-1-with-15-million/#6718a0a7713.

Berry, Jo. *Lilly Singh: The Unofficial Superwoman Guide.* London, UK: Trapeze Books, 2017.

DeMers, Jayson. "7 Reasons to Start a YouTube Channel Now (And the First Steps to Take)." *Forbes*, May 30, 2018. https://www.forbes.com/sites/jaysondemers/2018/05/30/7-reasons-to-start-a-youtube-channel-now-and-first-steps-to-take.

Fairley, James Dean. "The Pros and Cons of YouTube Business Marketing." LinkedIn, March 31, 2015. https://www.linkedin.com/pulse/pros-cons-youtube-business-marketing-james-dean-fairley.

Forbes. "Top Influencers of 2017." https://www.forbes.com/top-influencers.

France-Presse, Agence. "YouTube Star Lilly Singh to Be First Female US Late-Night Talk Show Host in Decades." *Jakarta Post*, March 19, 2019. https://www.thejakartapost.com/life/2019/03/18/youtube-star-lilly-sing-to-be-first-female-us-late-night-talk-host-in-decades.html.

Griffin, Louise. "Lilly Singh Says Farewell to 'Superwoman' Nickname After Triumphant YouTube Comeback." Metro.co.uk, January 11, 2019. https://metro.co.uk/2019/01/11/lilly-singh-says-farewell-to-superwoman-nickname-after-triumphant-youtube-comeback-8335473.

Gutelle, Sam. "Female YouTube Stars Join Lilly Singh to Promote #GirlLove." Tubefilter.com, December 29, 2015. https://www.tubefilter.com/2015/12/29/lilly-singh-girl-love-campaign.

Ibrahim, Banu. "Lilly Singh Gets Real About Being One of Few Viral South Asian YouTubers." AOL.com, June 9, 2016. https://www.aol.com/article/2016/06/09/lilly-singh-gets-real-about-being-one-of-few-viral-south-asian-y/21392420.

Jha, Rega. "14 Things We Learned When We Hung Out with Lilly 'Superwoman' Singh." BuzzFeed India, March 23, 2015. https://www.buzzfeed.com/regajha/o-m-g-l-o-l.

Lakshmin, Deepa. "Exactly 70 People Watched Lilly Singh's First YouTube Video—Now Millions Do." *MTV News*, October 21, 2015. http://www.mtv.com/news/2342360/lilly-singh-iisuperwomanii-youtube-interview.

Landau, Emily. "Lilly Singh Goes to Hollywood." *Toronto Life*, March 21, 2017. https://torontolife.com/city/life/inside-dizzying-world-lilly-singh-torontos-accidental-megastar.

Lewis, Casey. "This Is What Lilly Singh Wishes She Knew at Age 18." *TeenVogue*, October 20, 2015. https://www.teenvogue.com/story/lilly-singh-superwoman-advice-to-teens.

BIBLIOGRAPHY

Mankani, Sneha. "Superwoman on How to Become a YouTube Superstar." *Vogue India*, March 17, 2015. https://www.vogue.in/content/superwoman-how-become-youtube-superstar/.

O'Connor, Clare. "Forbes Top Influencers: How YouTuber Lilly Singh Is Going Mainstream—And Making Millions." *Forbes*, June 20, 2017. https://www.forbes.com/sites/clareoconnor/2017/06/20/forbes-top-influencers-lilly-singh-superwoman-youtube.

OpenQuotes. "Lilly Singh Quotes." https://openquotes.github.io/authors/lilly-singh-quotes.

Schomer, Stephanie. "Lilly Singh Conquered YouTube: Now She's Taking On Hollywood." *Entrepreneur*, March 4, 2019. https://www.entrepreneur.com/article/328067.

Singh, Lilly. *How to Be a Bawse: A Guide to Conquering Life*. New York, NY: Ballantine Books, 2017.

Singh, Lilly. "I'll See You Soon…" YouTube, November 12, 2018. https://www.youtube.com/watch?v=5OfFk5c01o.

Singh, Lilly. "This Channel Is Changing." YouTube, January 9, 2019. https://www.youtube.com/watch?v=VdkoPi04YbE.

Singh, Lilly. *Toxic Relationships: How to DE-TOX from Negative People and Abusive Relationships*. CreateSpace, 2017.

Spangler, Todd. "Top YouTuber Lilly Singh Says She's Taking a Break from Videos, Citing Mental Health." *Variety*, November 13, 2018. https://variety.com/2018/digital/news/lilly-singh-youtube-hiatus-videos-mental-health-1203027711.

Spangler, Todd. "YouTube Star Lilly Singh Comes Out as Bisexual, Gets Outpouring of Support." *Variety*, February 25, 2019. https://variety.com/2019/digital/news/lilly-singh-bisexual-youtube-1203148535.

Srinivasan, Madhumita. "From Lilly Singh to Superwoman." *Hindu*, April 12, 2015. https://www.thehindu.com/features/metroplus/from-lilly-singh-to-superwoman/article7093042.ece.

Stych, Anne. "Olay Spotlights Fearless Women in 'Face Anything' Campaign." Bizwomen.com, August 15, 2018. https://www.bizjournals.com/bizwomen/news/latest-news/2018/08/fearless-women-star-in-olays-face-anything.html?page=all.

Upadhyay, Karishma. "YouTube Superstar Lilly Singh Shares Secrets of Success in New Book." asiaone.com, May 12, 2017. https://www.asiaone.com/showbiz/youtube-superstar-lilly-singh-shares-secrets-success-new-book.

Winn, Scott, director. *A Trip to Unicorn Island.* FilmBuff, 2014.

INDEX

A

advertisers/sponsors, 23–24

B

Buckle, Allen, 18

C

collaborations, 20, 24, 29, 34–35

D

depression, 6, 11, 14, 26

F

Face Anything, 33
Fahrenheit 451, 37

G

#GirlLove, 32
Gomez, Selena, 11, 23, 29

H

Helbig, Grace, 23, 29, 33
How to Be a Bawse: A Guide to Conquering Life, 4, 31, 33
Humble the Poet, 17, 29

I

Ice Age: Collision Course, 37

K

Khan, Shah Rukh, 21

L

"#LEH," 17
Little Late Night with Lilly Singh, A, 6, 37
Los Angeles, 10, 22–23, 24

M

Marbles, Jenna, 11–12, 29

R

Rock, the, 9, 29

S

Sikhism, 8
Singh, Lilly
  awards and recognition, 30, 33
  books, 4, 31–32
  childhood and education, 7–11
  and critics, 35
  first video, 12
  philanthropy, 6, 32–33
  YouTube channel and career, 4, 13–18, 19–24, 25–29, 34–37
Singh, Tina, 7
Smith, Will, 29, 35
Stirling, Lindsey, 33
IISuperwomanII, 4, 6, 13, 16, 18, 19, 20, 21, 23, 30, 31, 34
Superwoman Vlogs, 20

T

Team Super, 21, 30, 34
Toxic Relationships: How to De-Tox from Negative People and Abusive Relationships, 32
Trip to Unicorn Island, A, 27, 30
Trip to Unicorn Island, A, tour, 4, 26–27

U

UNICEF, 6, 33

Y

YouTube, tips for starting, 17, 22

ABOUT THE AUTHOR

Henrietta Toth began writing middle-grade nonfiction following a twenty-year career as an editor in academic publishing. She has learned a lot by working on books about many different topics. Now she has learned a lot about YouTube. This is her second book in the Top YouTube Stars series.

PHOTO CREDITS

Cover, p. 1 Noam Galai/WireImage/Getty Images; pp. 4–5 Brandon Williams/Getty Images; pp. 8, 25, 27 FilmMagic/Getty Images; p. 9 Kathy Hutchins/Shutterstock.com; p. 12 Michael Bezjian/WireImage/Getty Images; p. 14 Emma McIntyre/Getty Images; p. 16 Rob Kim/FilmMagic/Getty Images; p. 20 Frazer Harrison/Getty Images; p. 21 Mail Today/India Today Group/Getty Images; pp. 23, 30 Kevin Winter/Getty Images; p. 32 Kelly Sullivan/Getty Images; p. 34 Sajjad Hussain/AFP/Getty Images; p. 36 Angela Weiss/AFP/Getty Images.

Design: Michael Moy; Layout: Ellina Litmanovich; Editor: Xina M. Uhl; Photo Researcher: Nicole DiMella